PURE SHOCK VALUE

Matt Pelfrey

I0139745

BROADWAY PLAY PUBLISHING INC
224 E 62nd St, NY, NY 10065
www.broadwayplaypub.com
info@broadwayplaypub.com

First printing: December 2011
I S B N: 978-0-88145-517-5

Book design: Marie Donovan
Page make-up: Adobe Indesign
Typeface: Palatino
Printed and bound in the U S A

The world premier of PURE SHOCK VALUE was from 27 February-22 March 2009, produced by Killing My Lobster (produced by Sarah Mitchell & Michael Hoch) at the Exit Theater, San Francisco, CA. The cast and creative contributors were:

GABBY .... Erin Carter
TEX .... Justin Lamb
ETHAN .... Chris Yule
JULIAN..Calum Grant

Director ....Laley Lippard

CHARACTERS

ETHAN
TEX
GABBY
JULIAN

ACT ONE

(A shape on the couch, hidden under a blanket, quietly and intensely masturbates to Field of Dreams *playing on the television. And then, after a disturbing moment or two...)*

*(*TEX *bursts in through the front door—)*

ETHAN: —HEY!

TEX: Is she here—?

ETHAN: —JESUS, MAN! —Where is she?

*(*ETHAN *sits up, keeps himself covered by the sheet.* TEX *doesn't bat an eye at* ETHAN's *self-manipulation.)*

ETHAN: YOU MIND??

TEX: Gabby??

ETHAN: Tex, you ass—

TEX: *(Points to bedroom)* Gabb? Yo! Gabsters? *(He rushes into the bedroom. A moment later he comes out.)* What the fuck?

ETHAN: How 'bout knocking?

TEX: It's almost midnight!? What gives?

ETHAN: Do NOT barge in like that—

TEX: You want privacy when pulling your pud, lock the door.

ETHAN: You busted it—!

TEX: So fix it!

ETHAN: —This morning!

TEX: Whatever. I need answers. Are we millionaires yet? Do I have a career? Am I a real person?

ETHAN: I don't know.

TEX: AM I A REAL PERSON?

ETHAN: I DON'T KNOW YOU ANNOYING ASSHOLE!

TEX: Page her ass...

ETHAN: Sit down.

TEX: Not my style.

ETHAN: When she's done, first thing she'll do is call.

TEX: You think...?

ETHAN: Trust me.

TEX: Why?

ETHAN: Because, I've been making sweet, gentle, yet intense love to her for three-and-a-half years. That makes me an expert on how she operates.

TEX: Screw it— *(Whips out his cell)*

ETHAN: —Don't!

TEX: —Deeds, not words, baby... *(Hits "call" on his cell.)*

ETHAN: Nice, interrupt the meeting. Smooth...

TEX: —Chill thy self. I'm taking control of a— *(Beat. Listens. Gets voice mail)* Goddamn it... *(Beat)* ...Voice mail's full.

ETHAN: Could have told you that.

TEX: Oh, cause you've tried to call her already?

ETHAN: Of course.

TEX: You sick son-of-a-bitch. *(Puts his cell away)*

ETHAN: Now sit down a sec, we gotta have some words...

TEX: Maybe we can drive to the restaurant...

ETHAN: Tex, for serious, there's something—

TEX: —Where's the meeting? It's possible they're having drinks—

ETHAN: Hey!

TEX: What?

ETHAN: I'm proposing after she gets here with the good news.

TEX: Hardy har-har. *(Sees he's serious)* What?

ETHAN: Yeah. So, that means at some point, after we celebrate, I'll give you the signal to clear out.

TEX: Please be joking.

ETHAN: ...No joke.

TEX: I said: PLEASE BE JOKING!

ETHAN: I'm proposing. Yep. Exactly what I'm doing...

TEX: Why?

ETHAN: Getting the vibe she wants The Big Ring so I figure what the hell? Throw her bone. She's a good kid.

TEX: You're on the cusp of launching a major directing career and you're gonna let yourself get attached?

ETHAN: How many times has dad been married?

TEX: Excellent point. However, the old man has done one thing his entire life: sell used cars in Austin. He's never been on the verge of big time H-Town success. He's never had a shot at ungodly collateral pussy. Actress pussy! Or even better: hot, wannabe actress pussy, which we all know is as hot as actress pussy but with the essence of desperation mixed in...which is super hot.

ETHAN: What do you want me to say? I love her. As sad and twisted as that may sound, it's the truth.

TEX: You love Gabby.

ETHAN: I love her.

TEX: Gabby.

ETHAN: Yeah.

TEX: Our Gabby.

ETHAN: Yes, dick.

TEX: You love her...?

ETHAN: That's what I said.

TEX: Love, love...

ETHAN: Enough! Forget about it! Forget I said anything! *(He gets up—he's wearing boxers. He also has an erection, but it's noticeably small.)* Now, in the meantime, you wanna finish this off for me? I mean, since Gabby isn't here.

TEX: Sicko.

ETHAN: Prude.

TEX: I'm your little brother. And for the record, unlike you, I'm not bi-curious.

ETHAN: Neither am I. Gonna make you wear a mop on your head, you could've done it prison style. I'd just shut my eyes and pretend you're that chick from *Atonement.*

TEX: I should get hypno-therapy. I bet at some point in our childhood, you fondled me.

ETHAN: You should be so lucky. It'd give you something real to write about besides farts.

TEX: Farts are gonna make you a very rich man.

ETHAN: Better hope so.

(ETHAN *wanders into the bathroom.* TEX *does really bad Tai Chi while talking to* ETHAN, *off stage.*)

TEX: Got any cold meds in there?

ETHAN: *(From bathroom)* Why? Coming down with something?

TEX: Hell no. I just need the stuff to fuel my pulsating talent. Normally, I'm a totalfuckinggenius. That's an established fact. But when I get a nice pseudophed buzz, a little taste of that non-drowsy action, I totally become this Shane Black-meets David Mamet-meets-Julian Quintana-meets-that guy who wrote Chinatown. It's like my normal writing but with chives. You see, what normally'd be just a metaphorical baked potato, becomes a baked potato with chives.

(No response from ETHAN. *Maybe just the distant sound of him pissing. No worries,* TEX'*s scattered attention span moves to* Field of Dreams *playing on the T V.)*

TEX: Okay, I need to know this: what's your deal with *Field of Dreams*? Seems like an odd choice for stroke material. Plus, I don't remember you being a big Costner fan.

*(*ETHAN *enters from the bathroom. Thankfully, he's no longer engorged.)*

TEX: Seriously, what's even slightly erotic about this flick? I mean, James Earl Jones? Talk about a bone kill...

ETHAN: It's the corn. *(He throws a pack of cold meds to* TEX.*)* Here. Rock out.

TEX: Sweet. *(He goes into the kitchenette, finds a dirty glass, rinses it out, gets some tap water and downs three or four cold tablets. As he does the above:)* Enjoy your last moments on planet Earth as a loser, 'cause when Gabby gets back, you'll be instantly transformed into one of the Beautiful People. That's right: the privileged. We can act like arrogant, smug, self-satisfied pricks 'cause our ship's gonna come in. And y'know what you get to do when that happens...?

(While the above goes on, ETHAN searches the floor for pants. He finds some grubby jeans. Puts them on)

ETHAN: You need a beer.

TEX: You get to fuck with people...

ETHAN: Want a beer?

TEX: Engage in full-contact debauchery and nobody cares.

ETHAN: I got some Pabst left—

TEX: You get to throw your weight around—

ETHAN: —Yes or no?

TEX: —Pay back every chick who's dumped you. Yes, beer. Everyone I know who's pissed me off, dissed my shit, they're gettin' a tap on the shoulder. It's a mass e-mail blast of FUCK YOU'S! A to goddamn Z. Not even an individual "fuck you". That's too good. I'm sending a bulk, impersonal "kiss my ass" spam. Then I'll change all my contact info, 'cause I'll be reborn. The grand woman named Hollywood is gonna spread wide and I'm popping out. *(Beat)* You should call Keely. Get some of her killer Hydro.

ETHAN: Let's stay focused.

TEX: Easier with the proper substance. The K-babe has a wide selection.

ETHAN: No.

TEX: She can hook us up with something to take the edge off. We all don't do the Zen-Stroke. Some of us are normal and need druggage.

ETHAN: —Forget it.

TEX: You're lucky enough to live five houses down from the—

ETHAN: I said no—

TEX: —the most discreet, most un-fucked up dealer of contraband this side of Silverlake and you don't wanna—

ETHAN: NOT TONIGHT. Wait for Gabby. Find out where we stand in the cosmos.

TEX: If you'd just let go and think more positive, we'd all be further along...

ETHAN: Spare me...

TEX: Seriously, you gotta get your mind in the zone...

ETHAN: What zone...?

TEX: ...the zone-zone. The zone-place where, where fucking world domination rocks the mic...

ETHAN: I don't know what that means...I barely know what anything you say means.

TEX: Running up the steps? Gonna fly now? "Yo, Adrian, I did it!" Right?

ETHAN: No. Not right.

TEX: What's your bug? I'm givin' you pearls here—

ETHAN: Fincher was twenty-seven when he made those kick-ass commercials and all the Madonna videos...

TEX: So?

ETHAN: He was twenty-nine when he shot *Alien 3*.

TEX: And it sucked so hard—

ETHAN: —The point is: I'm fucking behind. Way way behind. I'm nowhere near where I should be.

TEX: Behind what?

ETHAN: I'm thirty-five years old. I'm in an advance stage of artistic decay as far as the Industry is concerned. I should be on my fourth or fifth feature by now. This should be chapter five of my future biography!

TEX: How about Quintana?

ETHAN: What about him?

TEX: *(Nods at the* Where Rats Go To Die *poster)* Julian Quintana was twenty-nine when he shot *Where Rats Go To Die.*

ETHAN: You trying to make me feel like shit?

TEX: His first film and he hadn't done anything before that 'cept work in a fucking video store.

ETHAN: That would have been six years ago for me. You don't understand age...you're twenty five. You got at least four years before you die on the vine.

TEX: Age is in the mind.

ETHAN: Age is showing up every day on my face. I got "dad wrinkles" here and here.

TEX: So get a face peel. Botox your ballsack.

ETHAN: Why would I Botox my balls?

TEX: Did you see that picture of Saddam in the jail cell? —His nuts were swinging down to his knees. That ain't right.

ETHAN: Whatever. My balls are the least of my worries.

TEX: After tonight, we're all gonna be calling the shots, living on a diet of bejewelled thongs and Red Bull. At least I will. You can buy Gabby a bejewelled thong if you want...

ETHAN: I don't blame you for being full of spunk. This is all new to you. But Gabby and I've been down this road. And what you don't get is every year after thirty you don't break through, odds skyrocket for becoming a Hollywood freak...giving it one more year over and over 'til there's no going back 'cause you have no real world skills, and you look in the mirror and, and you've become a grotesque...

TEX: —Like Angelyne!

ETHAN: —Exactly like Angelyne: Ten pounds of humanity encased in one-hundred pounds of silicone and make-up.

TEX: ...so, so gross!

ETHAN: —Driving around like a zombie in a pink Corvette.

TEX: Speaking of Hollywood monsters? Guess who I saw?

ETHAN: No legs? Homeless? Cleans stars on the Walk of Fame with a toothbrush?

TEX: No, no— But that guy seriously rocks. I mean, legless, homeless, eternally cleaning John Wayne's star on the walk of fame? That's a commitment to excellence. Fuck, I'm blanking on the name... You know who it is...help me...

ETHAN: "Cast me!" guy? Lives in that weird car covered with his head-shots and shit? Dennis something—Wood—?

TEX: *(Remembering)* Yes! Thank you. Dennis Woodruff! His skin looks like it's made of jerky.

ETHAN: How old's that dude?

TEX: Ancient. Fiftish...or shit, maybe even late fifties! He's a fucking mummy.

ETHAN: Angelyne and Dennis Woodruff—they should be crucified and left on the outskirts of town as a warning. Right there on the 101 and the 5.

TEX: "Abandon hope, all who enter."

ETHAN: The Patron Saints of Failed Hollywood Dreams.

(TEX *pulls out a small notebook and a pen.*)

TEX: That's sexy. I'm gonna use that in something. *(He whips out a small notebook and jots the line down when—)*

(GABBY *bursts through the front door.*)

TEX: Holy shit—!

ETHAN: Gabby!

(GABBY's *dressed in a sleek, no-nonsense power outfit that says "I'm hot but you better take me seriously, asshole."*)

TEX: About time!

ETHAN: What's up...?

TEX: What happened...?

ETHAN: Bad news...?

TEX: Talk, woman!

(GABBY *goes straight to the kitchen, gets a beer. Stares at them. Cracks it open. Takes a long drink)*

ETHAN: How'd it go?

TEX: Are we the new badboys on the block or what?

(GABBY *sits, stressed-out and tired.* TEX *hovers, expectant, unwilling to take her body language as a sign of bad news. She takes another long gulp.)*

ETHAN: So?

TEX: C'mon! How was the meeting?

GABBY: The meeting...

ETHAN: He did meet with you, right?

GABBY: Yeah. *(Long pause. She's still getting her thoughts together.)*

ETHAN: So...?

GABBY: We met, had dinner, discussed...

TEX: He like my script?

GABBY: Thought "Barking Spiders" was hilarious.

TEX: Clearly a man of taste.

GABBY: Said he and his partners were quoting lines from it for the past three days.

TEX: *(Enunciating clearly for effect)* Fuck yes, ladies and gentlemen: fuck. Yes.

GABBY: Said *Barking Spiders* would make *Super Bad* and *40 Year-old Virgin* seems like after school specials. The studios are hungry for "edgy" comedies and if they packaged this right it'd be "an easy lay".

TEX: Dude, I'm the king of "edgy". WAIT!

GABBY: What?

TEX: Are you giving me exact quotes?

GABBY: What're you talking about?

TEX: Are you paraphrasing or are you giving us exact quotes? Is that what he said or did he say it a different way?

GABBY: Why?

ETHAN: Yeah, what the fuck are you babbling about?

TEX: Just tell me: Did he say we were "huge talents?" It's important. Very fucking important.

GABBY: No, no, no.

TEX: No, what? C'mon! Huge talents. Yes, or no?

GABBY: He did not in any way, shape, or form, use the phrase "huge talents".

TEX: You're sure?

GABBY: Yes.

TEX: Okay, cool. That was fucking close.

ETHAN: Why?

TEX: Dude, everything in this town's a code. When you say someone is a "huge talent" you're saying they suck major ass. It just the accepted subtext. It's like wishing someone "the best of luck with their career." That's code for "I hope to see you selling oranges at the La Cienaga off ramp after your next movie bombs".

ETHAN: *(To* GABBY*)* Ignore him. Go on. Sounds like dinner went aces.

GABBY: Yep. Scheduled a meeting tomorrow at their Warner Brothers' crib. Said Donner films wanted to be in the *Barking Spiders* business.

TEX: WE MADE IT!! WE SO FUCKIN' MADE IT! *(He leaps. He dances. Is a celebratory moonwalk too much to ask?)*

ETHAN: Sit your shit down! Does she look like a woman who's "made it."

TEX: Gabby, c'mon, spill your load.

GABBY: We had it...

TEX: Yeah...?

GABBY: ...but I lost it.

TEX: Whoa, whoa, whoa, how's that?

*(*GABBY *just sits there, zoning out.)*

TEX: Dude, explain yourself!

GABBY: I wouldn't...

TEX: What?

GABBY: I wouldn't fuck him.

ETHAN: He...wanted to sleep with you?

GABBY: Did I say sleep? No. He wanted to fuck, Ethan. Fuck.

(Pause. GABBY *stares at* ETHAN, *trying to gage his reaction.)*

TEX: Okay. Hold on: Did he hit on you or was this like, something he was using as—

GABBY: We finished dinner and he said to me, quote — wait, I'm not gonna repeat it.

TEX: Hey, come on! This is our careers here! Full disclosure!

GABBY: No way. I'm not gonna humiliate myself any more. The point is, as we were leaving, he made a very crude, disgusting suggestion and made no attempt to hide the fact that the deal was contingent on me being his human blow-up doll.

TEX: He knows you and Ethan are together, right?

GABBY: So?

TEX: Maybe he was joking?

GABBY: He wasn't joking.

TEX: But how do you know?

GABBY: Because I know, Tex.

TEX: So, okay. You slapped him and left? Is that what we're—

GABBY: I didn't slap him... *(Beat)* ...and I didn't leave.

ETHAN: *(Worried)* Okay...

GABBY: I went to his car.

TEX: Oh, shit.

GABBY: It's...ah....yeah...

(An awkward pause)

ETHAN: Gab...Did you...?

GABBY: No...not really....

TEX: So there you go! No big deal! What the fuck are we angsting about? Let's get them back on the phone and patch shit up.

ETHAN: Tex—shut up for a second! *(Beat)* So you went to his car but you didn't do anything?

GABBY: Yeah.

ETHAN: For once I gotta agree with Tex, what's the big problem?

GABBY: Because I almost did, alright? I had to catch myself. Can you believe that? What the fuck's wrong with me? That I'd entertain even the suggestion? That I didn't spit in the guy's face and grind my knee into his groin when he purred those words into my ear. I went out to his car. I got in. *(Pause)* I...kissed his disgusting, garlicky mouth...I...

ETHAN: Okay, wait: So now the story is you kissed him...?

GABBY: Yeah.

(GABBY watching ETHAN as he considers the ramifications of this. It's impossible to tell how he's taking it.)

(TEX breaks the moment—)

TEX: *(As much to ETHAN as GABBY)* So, you pulled back. Kissing's no biggie. A little tongue. Swap a little spit...maybe you gave his hotdog a grip—we're all adults. No harm, no foul. It's not like you gargled his chowder.

GABBY: You don't get it, do you?

TEX: There's nothing to get! You gave him a peck on the cheek. The only person who should care here is Ethan, and he's cool. Look at him. He doesn't mind. We all good, baby.

GABBY: Ethan?

(ETHAN takes a moment before answering...)

ETHAN: You just kissed. Hey, so what, right?

GABBY: You're not pissed...or jealous...?

ETHAN: Honestly, at this point in the Great Struggle, if it'd get our movie made, I'd probably beg you to sleep with the guy. I mean...right?

GABBY: You...really mean that?

(ETHAN doesn't really, but now that GABBY's asking, he gives it a moment of real thought.)

ETHAN: If it actually got us some action from a legitimate production company? Some seed money? A chance for us to make a movie? *(Another moment of consideration)* If you'd be good with it, I'd roll with it.

(GABBY's pretty stunned by that, and it shows for a second, but she does her best to compose.)

GABBY: Oh.

(A pause. TEX jumps to try and keep things on track:)

TEX: The bottom line is, this guy was rude and inappropriate to my brother's fiancée. But that's no reason to scuttle any potential deal. He's just a big kid. That's how guys are in this town. Just big, spoiled kids used to getting what they want and feeling important. Now, focus a second here Gab: Do we still have the meeting tomorrow?

ETHAN: Tex...

TEX: No, really...

GABBY: We don't have the meeting anymore. *(Beat)* Did you say fiancée?

TEX: But he thinks *Barking Spiders* is brilliant.

ETHAN: Tex...

TEX: What?

ETHAN: We're gonna have to eat this one. It's a loss. Let it go.

TEX: No fucking way. I refuse.

GABBY: Tex. Why'd you call me Ethan's fiancée? *(Turns to* ETHAN*)* Why'd he say that?

TEX: *(Off-handed)* Ethan was gonna propose tonight if we got a deal.

ETHAN: I'm never telling you jack-shit again you little fuck roach.

TEX: You didn't say it was a secret.

ETHAN: Pull your head outta your ass.

GABBY: Is this true? You were gonna propose?

ETHAN: Um, kinda, yeah.

GABBY: You...you bought me a ring?

ETHAN: ...ring?

GABBY: ...yeah, I mean...

ETHAN: Not really...

GABBY: Then...how—?

TEX: He said it was gonna be your reward for sealing the deal.

GABBY: My reward?

ETHAN: *(After a glare at* TEX*)* It's kinda like a reward, isn't it? I mean, you want to get married, right?

GABBY: Yes, but I don't want it to be my fucking "reward"!

TEX: Kids, kids, before we take a dark tour through the ninth circle of relationship hell, can we get back to the real issue—

GABBY: There is no real issue...it's fucking over. This was our only real lead and it's dead and buried.

TEX: There's still that assistant at Dreamworks.

GABBY: Fuck Dreamworks...

TEX: Hey! Hey! Hey! Shhhhhh!

GABBY: They're not the N S A. They're not listening in!

TEX: Just, come on...be cool.

GABBY: I don't give a shit anymore. I'm not worried about pissing off the Gods of Dreamworks or...Sony or Paramount. It doesn't matter at this point...just doesn't matter.

ETHAN: What's that mean?

GABBY: I was on the edge of the abyss tonight. I had a chance to peek into the murky depth of my soul. To see how much build-up, how much creepy looking fungus is growing there. It was...disgusting.

TEX: We need Keely. We need hard drugs.

GABBY: What I need is to move to a real city or...hell, anywhere. Maybe even back home.

TEX: You're being hysterical.

GABBY: I'm moving back to Seattle.

ETHAN: You don't wanna do that.

GABBY: Maybe I do.

ETHAN: So your asshole dad can laugh in your face? Tell you what an idiot you were to move here? Or maybe the idea of flushing another three years down the toilet while you take care of your grandma sounds fun. Nothing like cleaning out a colostomy bag while you're cussed-out in Portuguese.

GABBY: Then San Francisco. Or New York.

ETHAN: There's nothing for you in San Francisco.

TEX: And what're you gonna do in New York, walk around and be "edgy" all day? Screw that. This is the new Center Of The Universe! It's the Pacific Century!

ETHAN: Tex is right. L A's the place you belong. Also, there's no way in hell I'm moving away, so... No L A, no Ethan.

(ETHAN *expects that to have an impact.* GABBY *just kind of looks at him and gives him a slight courtesy nod to acknowledge his statement.*)

TEX: I'm sorry you got felt up, Gab, but you're kind of acting like a twelve-year-old here. It's no big deal. We're having a minor setback. Don't make it more than it is.

GABBY: If you caught yourself about to let this guy do things to you, you'd be examining your life too!

TEX: That's not an accurate comparison. A similar thing would be if, like, an older development chick demanded I put out quality meat for her.

ETHAN: Would you?

TEX: To get *Barking Spiders* made? Shit yes! I mean within reason. I admit, anything over thirty-eight might take some serious soul searching, but the point is, I'm totally committed to this project!

GABBY: And I'm not?

TEX: All I'm saying is you don't have any options, so stop struggling. Leaving L A is a non-starter. The only reason not to put a glass dome over Hollywood and gas the rest of the planet is there wouldn't be anyone left to watch our films. Nothing out there matters. Plus, what do you think everyone's doing in these other cities? They're working on screenplays. Or they're thinking about working on a screenplay. Or they're reading a book on how to write a screenplay. Or they're working on something else they're hoping gets turned into a screenplay. Boom. Truth bomb. Shrapnel everywhere.

GABBY: It's a big world, Tex. Lot's of things going on. You might surprise yourself.

TEX: It's all just movie fodder. What's important about Rwanda? Don Cheadle's Oscar nom. The Holocaust?

Shindler's List. Nine-Eleven? A chance for Oliver Stone to do something heart-felt and Nick Cage to work his puppy eyes.

GABBY: You are a complete lunatic.

TEX: And you love it.

GABBY: I would actually like to have a family some day. A baby. Live with a little dignity. I really, really don't want to spend another five years desperately covering spec scripts in some shitty Hollywood apartment that smells like cat shit and week-old Taco Bell! I mean—

ETHAN: —All artist face this kind of self-doubt. This kind of struggle. You gotta just punch through. We've talked about this—

GABBY: —I'm sorry: "artists"?

TEX: Hey, Gabbs, speak for yourself. I'm a total artist! Fuckin' *Barking Spiders*! I can see the *New York Times* review now: "A trenchant, gastronomical satire." And I don't even know what trenchant means!

ETHAN: *(To* TEX*)* We need Keely. Get some Oki Green, blast away...

GABBY: I'm gonna go home and carbo-load.

ETHAN: No, no—stay. Please...

TEX: Yeah, mellow. Trust me, there's nothing in the world that can't be healed by a twelve pack of King Cobra and a pound of Trail Mix.

GABBY: We're part of the ninety-nine percent that come to this town and crash against the rocks. The one percent—the Kevin Smiths, the Coens, the Julian Quintana's of the world...they're out there somewhere...breathing different air, living in a completely different version of Los Angeles... full of different streets with entirely different names, different buildings...different people. We're a billion miles away from whatever fantasy world "Entourage" is talking about.

TEX: I ain't buying this shit. What you need for world domination is fucking talent and raw, throbbing intensity. And I got a colon-load of both. I'm as committed to total excellence now as ever.

GABBY: You're young.

TEX: Just not a quitter. And I'm a fucking genius.

(A festering lull)

(ETHAN *exits into the bathroom.)*

(TEX *sighs, sips at his beer, deep in thought.)*

(Then—a loud crash from outside. Something knocked over in ETHAN's *back yard—)*

GABBY: The hell...? *(She moves to investigate.)*

TEX: Maybe we just need to change direction.

GABBY: *(At the sliding glass door, peering into the dark.)* How so?

TEX: We blew ten grand on a short. We should do a feature for that amount—fuckin' digital, send it out on the web. *Blair Witch! Session 9! Chuck and Buck!*

(No more sounds. GABBY *steps away from the sliding glass door—)*

GABBY: Unfortunately, I don't have another grandmother who can die and leave me ten grand to piss away, and Ethan can't even pay to fix his back or his car, and you clearly have no money in your future, so it's all just—forget about it.

TEX: Nah, listen. This idea is so fucking kick-ass it'll attract money and talent. And this movie will have only one goal: To create a buzz, a stir, whatever. Make waves, a tsunami! If it ends up being a good film, hell, that's just chives.

(ETHAN *enters from bathroom.*)

ETHAN: What's he babbling about now...?

TEX: I'm saying we make a movie designed just to get attention... Obviously, it can't be bad, but it must have something else...that electricity, that X-factor, some shock value.

ETHAN: Like a Julian Quintana movie?

TEX: Exactly. Like Julian Quintana's first flick.

ETHAN: *Where Rats Go To Die.*

TEX: The way he used the ironic juxtaposition of humor with violence!

ETHAN: The finger cutting sequence? "One little piggy..." Slice! "Two little piggys..." Slice! "Three little piggy..."

TEX: Something like that! Bad intentions. Cut through the crowd. Plus, critics like that shit. They'll crap on something like *Barking Spiders* because it dares to be just funny. But if you throw violence in with the funny, you've got a volatile gumbo.

GABBY: Guys, *Rats* came out in the 90s. You can't out-shock the torture flicks that're getting crapped out these days.

TEX: I'm just saying we need to take the soul of what Julian did and learn from it—do the equivalent for now: Fuck everyone, just pursue your intense, singular vision. But it's gotta be jarring. Rattle the cage. Just give the entire film industry a big "fuck you, deal with us!" I mean, if Scorsese had to make a first film now, what would he do for impact?

GABBY: Have fun guys. Knock yourselves out.

TEX: Gabby, come on! This isn't you! We have to rally.
We can't slink into the night all defeated an' shit.
(Climbs up on a chair or the couch) We don't leave here
without a new plan of attack. Hey, remember when
Bill Pullman has that inspiring speech in *Independence
Day*? Where he gets the troops all ready to fight against
insurmountable odds? Close your eyes and pretend I
just said something that good.

GABBY: The last thing I want to do is sit around
brainstorming film ideas.

TEX: You don't have to: I already got one. And it's full
of tasty shock value.

GABBY: I don't wanna hear it.

TEX: It's been incubating in my melon for months.

GABBY: Well, keep it there.

TEX: No, this is great. Remember that psycho who got
busted 'cause he wanted to make Steven Spielberg his
sex slave?

GABBY: Cut! Stop! Thank you. I've already heard
enough.

TEX: No, really, he was stalking him. Had duct tape
and a ball-gag in the trunk of his car. Distributed a
newsletter on the internet called *Predators Monthly*.
Ugly-ass-shit. Dude, it was all over "Entertainment
Tonight."

GABBY: *(Overlaps from "Distributed...")* Stop, stop, stop,
stop, STOP!!

TEX: Listen! We buy the rights to his life, make a movie
about him. Fictional, we heighten everything. We make
it, like, a daring expose of toxic fame and obsession.
One man's attempt to penetrate, literally, the American
dream of Hollywood success. We can get someone
ultra cool to play the sicko: I'm thinking along the lines

of Crispen Glover. We'll call it *Fisting Spielberg*. *(Total fucking silence) Fisting Spielberg. (Beat)* Anyone? *(Beat)* Hello? *(Beat)* It's just a working title.

(ETHAN and GABBY stare at TEX like he's the biggest dick in the world.)

TEX: C'mon, it's brilliant. A bold *Taxi Driver* for a new millennium. We don't have to use Spieldberg's real name. We can call him...Stanley Spielburgler...

GABBY: Do you have even a single brain cell left?

TEX: It's genius, bro! Seething genius. I defy you to tell me otherwise!

ETHAN: We are NOT making a movie about the demented nut-job who wanted to ASS-BANG the man who gave the world *E T*!!!

TEX: Why not?

ETHAN: That is not how one goes about getting a fruitful and productive career in Hollywood.

TEX: You guys question whether you're artists or not, bag on *Barking Spiders*, but when I piss you an edgy, provocative concept, you both turn into lightweights.

ETHAN: We'd be black-listed. You don't pick a fight with the

most powerful man in the business you'd like to be in.

TEX: You wanna be maverick filmmakers or industry dick suckers?

GABBY: How'd you like to get stalked, okay, then have some snot-nosed brat make a movie about it?

TEX: Hey, life's tough when you're a public figure.

GABBY: The man has kids, a wife...this isn't a laughing matter.

TEX: If he actually was raped and his family hurt, then you'd be right. Totally off limits. However, you're wrong, the IDEA of a guy wanting to rape Steven Spielberg is funny. Maybe not funny ha-ha but still...

GABBY: Get your moral compass in shape!

TEX: If you guys were for real, the last thing you'd worry about is hurting some multimillionaire's feelings.

GABBY: Whatever. I don't give a shit what you have against Spielberg. I'm not gonna become a hyena and feed off of this celebrity's horrible experience just to get attention. Especially someone who's given the world so many great films.

(GABBY *gets up, walks towards the bathroom.* TEX *follows her saying the following:)*

TEX: Excuse me? Always? *1941? Amistad? Hook?* The last two Indy movies? I could go on; I won't.

(GABBY *exits to the bathroom and shuts the door in* TEX's *face.)*

TEX: His work has no subtext. It's exactly what it seems. He's one of the most overrated film directors in history!

GABBY: *(From inside the bathroom)* This is from a guy who writes fart jokes.

TEX: Aristophanes wrote fart jokes!

(TEX *turns to see* ETHAN *just staring at him.)*

TEX: Aristophanes lived back in the toga days.

(Off ETHAN's *cold stare)*

TEX: What?

ETHAN: You fucked up.

TEX: Which time?

ETHAN: Being my fiancée?

TEX: Yeah, I know, I know. My bad.

(ETHAN *suddenly punches* TEX *hard in the shoulder.*)

TEX: Owe! Fucker! Owe-shit!

ETHAN: You deserved it.

TEX: I know, but still. Fucking meow.

(ETHAN *gets his wallet out, pulls out some bills, hands them to* TEX.)

ETHAN: Here.

TEX: What's this?

ETHAN: Go to the corner, snatch us some more brew.

TEX: What kind?

ETHAN: Doesn't matter. Anything.

(TEX *nods, still massaging his shoulder.*)

ETHAN: And some Funyuns. For Gabby. She needs comfort food.

TEX: True enough. Back in a few.

(TEX *splits.* ETHAN *fixes the place up somewhat until* GABBY *enters from the bathroom.*)

GABBY: Tex go home?

ETHAN: A Captain Cork run. *(Silence)* Hey. C'mere.

(ETHAN *pulls* GABBY *into a hug. She doesn't put much effort into it.*)

ETHAN: I'm sorry.

GABBY: For what?

ETHAN: Tex wasn't supposed to say anything.

GABBY: Oh, you mean about your big marriage proposal? The one you were gonna do without a ring? That you were gonna do only if we got a deal? I mean, what is this shit?

ETHAN: It was like an impulsive thing. I was just thinking how great it would be—I'm sorry, alright?

Maybe I didn't think it through. Fine. *(A little too smooth:)* My heart was in the right place...

GABBY: So just because I want to get things straight, are you or are you not proposing to me tonight?

ETHAN: Well, now it just feels weird.

GABBY: So that's a no.

ETHAN: A tentative no.

(GABBY lets out a small, tired laugh at the total lameness of it all.)

GABBY: Fine. Whatever. *(She sits down somewhere, maybe the couch, and shuts her eyes.)* God. What are we doing here?

ETHAN: C'mon. You know exactly.

GABBY: You're right. I do. I manage the Kinkos on Sunset. I am a manager. Of a Kinkos. That's what I am. I am that. That is who I am. That is what I am.

ETHAN: Stop it. Don't go down that road.

GABBY: I'm not only going down that road, I own a house at the end of it. We all do. Tex is a studio page. You're a thirty-five year-old delivery boy and I'm a thirty-six year-old Kinkos manager. *(Beat)* I can't become one of those deluded trogs.

ETHAN: Which species of deluded trog are you referring to?

GABBY: Convinced I'm in the "business" just 'cause I happen to be in Los Angeles hustling a project and covering scripts part-time. I need to be making films. And if I can't actually do that, I don't wanna spend my life being close enough to smell it.

(GABBY puts her face in her hands. Is she crying? Probably not. Hard to tell. ETHAN sits next to her.)

ETHAN: Hey. It's okay. I fucked up. I'm sorry.

GABBY: For which?

ETHAN: The marriage thing.

GABBY: Right.

ETHAN: I handled the situation wrong. I would be lucky to marry you. Seriously. I'd be a lucky, lucky man if you'd have me. You're great. Yeah, maybe our situation here, working so hard, hustlin', it's hard to maybe make things as romantic as they could be. *(A long moment, then:)* You know what? I'm doing this. For real. I feel it, I'm doing it. Should I get on my knees? I will. *(He gets on his knees, holds her hand.)* Gabby Corrigan, will you ma—

GABBY: I blew him.

(Pause.)

ETHAN: What?

GABBY: I blew the guy.

(ETHAN gives GABBY a "W T F" look.)

GABBY: *(A little manic here)* I sucked his dick.

ETHAN: You're fucking with me.

GABBY: I'm so not. *(Harsh, but more like she's yelling these words to herself in a masochistic attempt to face the truth)* I sucked it! I SUCKED IT!

ETHAN: You're are fucking with me. You're unlike any woman I've ever met—and I mean that as a compliment.

GABBY: Ethan, I went out to this guy's car and I sucked his dick because he said it was the only way he'd guarantee to move our project up the ladder. *(Again, more inward, even though she's yelling)* I SUCKED HIS DICK!

ETHAN: You're not...?

GABBY: No.

ETHAN: You really...?

GABBY: Yes.

(Long pause)

ETHAN: Wow.

*(*GABBY *stares at* ETHAN. *Studying his expression.)*

GABBY: That doesn't make you totally pissed? Or are you now actually more impressed that I swallowed a bullet for the team?

ETHAN: I'm not sure.

GABBY: How's that marriage vibe feeling now?

ETHAN: Can I just like process this shit for a second?

(Agitated, GABBY *paces around the room.)*

GABBY: Maybe I am the type of person who'll end up getting giant breast implants and a million face-lifts. I mean, who would whore themselves out like I did? I'm disgusting. I'm every thing I hate about, like, a certain kind of woman. But that's me. I'm that person. On some weird existential level, I've damaged all woman-kind.

(Pause. Somewhere in the night, we hear the warped jingle from the ice cream truck trundling down El Centro. It's an extremely distorted—almost unrecognizable version of Hurray For Hollywood.*)*

GABBY: *(Distantly)* Midnight and there's an ice cream truck on duty. There's something vaguely creepy about that.

(Beat. The ice cream truck jingle fades into the night.)

ETHAN: So...if you did do what he asked... Why don't we have a meeting tomorrow? I mean, he asked for it, you did it. We should still be in play.

GABBY: I like how hard you're taking this.

ETHAN: What's done is done.

GABBY: Oh, okay. That's how it is!

ETHAN: Jesus, why are you ragging on me—you're the one who cheated!

GABBY: Yeah, and the way it's just shattered your world really tells me a lot!

ETHAN: Whatever. You're completely tripping out.

(GABBY *goes to the kitchen, finds some cheap whisky in a cupboard, pours some in a little Dixie cup and takes a shot.*)

ETHAN: Since we're already fighting, I seriously want to know. You gave him what he wanted. Where's our meeting?

(*Pause.*)

GABBY: When...I was done...he just laughed... Snickered, really. This really lame, privileged...snicker. Then he told me to get outta the car. Said he didn't have the authority to do anything for us. The guy... Aaron...he's not an executive...he's an intern.

ETHAN: Intern?

GABBY: Yeah. Our big, big make-or-break contact is just an intern.

ETHAN: Please, please, please be joking.

GABBY: Trust me: I wish.

ETHAN: An intern? A "fax this, grab the phone, mail this, cover this script" intern?

GABBY: Yep.

(ETHAN *seems to think really intensely for a moment.*)

GABBY: What're you doing?

ETHAN: Desperately searching for a bright side.

GABBY: There is none.

ETHAN: Okay—no, wait. Maybe as soon as he graduates from U S C, he'll blow up and—

GABBY: Not from U S C.

ETHAN: Okay, when he graduates from U C L A—

GABBY: Not from U C L A.

ETHAN: A F I?

GABBY: Nope.

ETHAN: Uh...

GABBY: Try Hollywood High.

ETHAN: No fucking way.

GABBY: And he's a sophomore.

ETHAN: How the—

GABBY: Hey, he fooled you too!

ETHAN: That's one tall sophomore...

GABBY: Yeah.

ETHAN: Jesus. I'm...I'm sorry.

GABBY: Not as sorry as me. I'M A WHORE! I'M A WHORE WHO DIDN'T EVEN GET A DEAL FOR BEING A WHORE! I'M A DISGUSTING DICK SUCKING KINKOS MANAGING WHORE. *(If she's not already on her feet and pacing around like a manic animal, she starts to do exactly that right now.)*

ETHAN: It's actually worse than that.

(GABBY spins to face him. Almost hysterical)

GABBY: Oh, really? I doubt it. I doubt in a million years it's worse than it already is. I'd love to hear it. Tell me. How THE FUCK is it worse than me being a total low-life whore?

ETHAN: Well. He was underage. That makes you a pedophile.

(The world stops.)

(Everything freezes.)

(A white square film projector light pops on GABBY *As the sound of a projector and a broken strip of film celluloid flapping rises.)*

(Everything but GABBY *in darkness)*

GABBY: *(Calm. Confiding in the audience. She's in her mind. Out of time and space)* Somewhere deep inside me, my soul vomits. I don't know if that's possible, even spiritually, but that's the only way I can describe this moment. My soul vomits all over itself. My spirit is rolling over and over in its own filth. I'm a monstrosity. A grotesque. Everything I thought about myself I see now was a lie. Or was true but was a smaller part of my life essence. Who I thought I was ran into a bigger shark, and that shark was the true me....a Kinkos managing whore slash pedophile. I am Angelyne and Dennis Woodruff's love child. I am a cheerleader mom trying to kill her daughter's competition. I'm the Hollywood skank who gets shot by Phil Specter. I'm the blond nitwit fucking OJ well after the big murder trial. I am the spiritual version of Meg Ryan's botched face-lift.

(In an instant, everything snaps back to normal. We continue as if the above never happened.)

GABBY: *(Re:* ETHAN'*s pedophile remark)* Holy shit. You're right. *(She wavers, dizzy, looks like she might blackout, then slumps down onto the floor.)*

GABBY: I'm a pedophile. My god.

*(*TEX *enters with a bag.)*

TEX: All our problems solved? We now have beer and Funyons for the little lady.

(TEX *throws the Funyuns at* GABBY, *then goes into the kitchen with the rest of the beers and stashes them in the fridge.*)

GABBY: *(Whisper)* Don't say shit to him.

ETHAN: No worries.

(TEX *comes back in slurping his beer.*)

TEX: *(To* GABBY*)* Feeling better yet? Ready to grab life by the hairy nads and yank?

(GABBY *just stares at* TEX. *All her carrying on has made her hair something close to a crazy mess.*)

TEX: My last offer: *Fisting Spielberg* could be the project that busts us into the stratosphere.

GABBY: If you ever mention *Fisting Spielberg* again, I might actually kill you.

(*Something about the way* GABBY *says that makes* TEX *wilt a bit.*)

TEX: Just...trying to save your creative soul.

GABBY: It's not yours to save.

TEX: Tell me what it'll take then.

ETHAN: Jesus, Tex, drop it already, please? Seriously, dude.

(GABBY *cracks open a brew takes a long drink.*)

GABBY: You wanna know what it'll take?

TEX: Yeah!

GABBY: You really wanna know?

TEX: I really wanna know.

GABBY: A fucking act of god you hyperactive twerp! Okay?? A sign from the heavens. Something so unbelievable and out there I would not believe it in a script and would instantly mark "pass" on the

coverage. Okay? Good enough? DO YOU HEAR ME?
DO YOU HEAR ME? AN ACT OF GOD!!

*(Suddenly there's another loud clanging sound from the
backyard. Like something big tumbled into a bunch of
garbage cans. TEX lights up, desperate for any thin reed to
hang his hopes on.)*

TEX: There it is!

GABBY: There what is?

TEX: You said you needed a sign. That was it.

GABBY: Ethan's ratty, skanky-ass dog knocking over
the cans wasn't what I had in mind!

ETHAN: Can't be Orson. He's at the vets.

TEX: Still has worms?

ETHAN: He's infested.

(Another crash!)

TEX: Then what was that?

ETHAN: I...uh...good question.

TEX: Maybe it's what's-his-name again—next door.

ETHAN: Can't be. Nacho's off the sauce.

GABBY: Get something.

ETHAN: Like?

GABBY: Hello? A weapon?

ETHAN: I don't got any.

TEX: If this was my pad, I'd be loading my shotgun
right now.

ETHAN: Wait a sec. *(He goes to his desk, gets his walking
cane.)* Here we go.

TEX: You got a pimp stick?

ETHAN: I found this on the street. Use it when my back
gets too bad.

TEX: Cool.

(Now they hear this sobbing in the back yard! It goes on for a moment or two, then mutates into this totally strange, pathetic, whimpering sound.)

ETHAN: Something's definitely out there.

(TEX grabs an empty beer bottle as a weapon. GABBY goes to the sliding glass door and peers out, but it's pitch black.)

GABBY: I can't see shit.

(GABBY tries the light switch. Not gonna happen. ETHAN finds a flashlight.)

GABBY: Outside light's out.

ETHAN: Yeah, I know. *(He opens the sliding glass door, shines the flashlight into the darkness.)* Hey! Come out of there! C'mon! *(To the others)* Someone's in the Doggloo.

(TEX joins ETHAN at the door.)

TEX: *(To mystery person)* Be cool, man. Get outta the Doggloo though. That's for canines only! *(To ETHAN)* Fucker's ensconced. Don't think he's coming. Flush him out.

ETHAN: How?

TEX: Garden hose.

ETHAN: WHAT?

TEX: You heard me. Squirt him down.

ETHAN: Think that's cool?

TEX: He's intruding!

GABBY: It might piss him off.

(ETHAN exits into the back yard.)

TEX: *(To ETHAN)* Just remember, he's on your property, legally you can do what you want to 'im.

GABBY: *(To ETHAN)* Careful.

(We hear the hose turn on...)

TEX: *(To* ETHAN*)* ...there you go...

GABBY: *(To* ETHAN*)* Back up if he goes berserk.

(...then the sound of water spraying against the Doggloo, a startled yelp from the mystery person.)

GABBY: Oh, he is all fucked up.

TEX: Yeah he is.

*(*GABBY *and* TEX *watch...and suddenly don't like what they see* ETHAN *doing.)*

GABBY: Wait— What?

TEX: Ethan! Don't! Stop that!

GABBY: —Don't touch him!

TEX: —Stop!

GABBY: —Ethan—!

TEX: —Don't...

GABBY: —Shit...

TEX: ...not inside you fucking idiot!

*(*GABBY *and* TEX *back away.* ETHAN *enters with the drenched homeless guy* [JULIAN]. *He is dirty, cut and bleeding, clothes torn. No shoes.)*

ETHAN: Help me here!

TEX: No way! I'm not touching him.

GABBY: Help him!

TEX: You!

GABBY: You're a guy!

TEX: Wrong: I'm a dude!

*(*GABBY *gives* TEX *a "W T F" look.)*

ETHAN: Somebody help me! He's slipping!

(GABBY *and* TEX *stare.* ETHAN *loses his grip. The homeless man thuds to the floor with an ugly grunt.)*

ETHAN: Thank you very fucking much!

TEX: What're you doing?

ETHAN: Guy's in trouble!

TEX: He's homeless! Respect his lifestyle choice!

GABBY: He's leaking!

TEX: It's gravy. Homeless Man gravy.

ETHAN: He needs our help. C'mon! Get over here!

TEX: Let the professionals handle it.

ETHAN: Someone beat him good. We gotta call the cops.

TEX: You realize this guy can sue you.

ETHAN: Tex - give me your cell.

TEX: You realize that don't you?

ETHAN: What?

TEX: You brought him into your house.

ETHAN: So?

TEX: Hosed him down...

ETHAN: Make your point!

TEX: For all we know this is imprisonment or something. You might have exposed yourself, legally speaking.

ETHAN: No way...

TEX: Helping people can be dangerous...

GABBY: He's got a point.

ETHAN: Well excuse me for having a conscience.

TEX: Don't get New Agey.

ETHAN: How's that New Agey?

TEX: Just sayin', don't rationalize making a stupid decision.

ETHAN: What should I've done?

TEX: Hosed him down as previously discussed, let him slink off into the night.

(The homeless man tries to crawl, rather pathetically, along the floor, making very little progress. It's more just a writhing motion, like he's swimming in place, with occasional gurgling sounds.)

GABBY: He's here now. What the hell do we do?

TEX: Put him back outside, let nature take its course.

ETHAN: That's fucking ethical. Soak a homeless man to the bone, then put him outside for the night.

JULIAN: Yuuuuuuuugggg...

(They stare at him.)

TEX: Bet he's got the flesh-eating bacteria. Incurable T B at the minimum.

ETHAN: How about I put him outside, then call the cops.

GABBY: I'm not lying to the police. What if they show up, we say one thing, and the guy gets rational or something and says we brought him inside?

TEX: Dudes, we're complicating things way too much. Here's the plan: Takes his wet shirt off, put a dry one on him, give him a blankie, send him outside. Problem solved.

(They watch him some more as he tries to crawl...with little success.)

ETHAN: Alright. Good enough. Let's do it. *(He exits.)*

TEX: Earth to homeless dude, can you hear me? Do you understand me?

JULIAN: ...Yuuuuuugggg...

(ETHAN *comes in with a shirt, an old blanket, and wearing rubber gloves.*)

TEX: *(Re: the gloves)* Good thinking.

ETHAN: Okay, back up, I'm gettin' this over with.

(ETHAN *pulls the homeless man's shirt off.*)

GABBY: *(Re: the homeless man's physique)* Not bad for a guy living on the street.

TEX: He is rather buff. I guess here, even the homeless wail on their abs.

(ETHAN *tries to put the dry shirt on his body, but the homeless man isn't cooperating.*)

GABBY: Great.

ETHAN: Tex, hold his arms.

TEX: In another life, brotha.

ETHAN: Help me out.

TEX: No way. I frown on body fluids.

ETHAN: Just, c'mon!

TEX: Forget the shirt, give him the blanket. It's not that cold.

(ETHAN *tries to force the homeless man's hands into the shirt, again he doesn't cooperate, pulling his hands away, etc. When the homeless man does this, he lets go of a pill bottle he has been, up to this point, clutching in his fist.* GABBY *goes to it, picks it up.*)

ETHAN: What's that?

GABBY: I'm looking. *(Sh reads the bottle.)* Oh my god.

TEX: What?

GABBY: No fucking way...

ETHAN: What?

GABBY: ...Impossible.

ETHAN: What is?

(*But* GABBY *is dumbstruck. She just stares at the homeless man.* ETHAN *goes to her, grabs the bottle from her and reads it.*)

ETHAN: (*Majorly stunned*) Shit...

(TEX *grabs the bottle and reads it, turns to the homeless man, stares...*)

ETHAN: It's...

GABBY: Yeah...

TEX: Holy ka-ka, it's really...I mean, that's...

(*It looks like they're all about to scream out his name, then the shock of what's fallen into their laps seems to sink in, they almost all visibly deflate...*)

GABBY: (*Soft*) Julian Quintana...

TEX: Julian-fucking Quintana.

ETHAN: In the bruised flesh.

GABBY: The hottest, hippest, edgiest, most ironic, most passionate filmmaking maverick on the face of planet earth...

TEX: A total, fucking, genius.

ETHAN: And he's secreting on my floor. I mean, that's my floor, that's Julian, and those're his fluids and they're all occupying the same point in space and time...right now!

GABBY: Get 'im to the couch!

TEX: Yeah, yeah—

(ETHAN *pulls off the gloves, throws them aside. He and* TEX *pick up* JULIAN *and drag him to the couch, sit him down.*)

TEX: Thought he looked familiar.

ETHAN: Bullshit you did.

TEX: Really! But with that stubble and dirt and blood—
I—but it's him...Julian Quintana. Look at these hands...
they typed *Where Rats Go to Die.*

(GABBY stares in shock.)

GABBY: ...oh god...

ETHAN: What?

GABBY: Oh. My. God.

TEX: What's with you?

GABBY: This...Tex, you were right...

TEX: Yeah? Cool. What about?

GABBY: It's a sign from God!

ETHAN: 'Course it is.

GABBY: You kidding me? He just shows up like this?

TEX: She's got a point. This is one hell of an argument
that the Big Man exists and has a keen interest in
Young Hollywood.

ETHAN: A sign from God would be if he just wandered
in here, totally normal and rational, and offered us a
three picture deal, with housekeeping.

TEX: I'd love a deal with "housekeeping". Our own
offices. Personal assistants!

*(GABBY backs away, truly, deeply, profoundly affected by
what's happened.)*

GABBY: This's scary...I mean it...I'm really really...
moved. *(Beat)* This means something.

TEX: *(To JULIAN)* Man, can I get your autograph?

ETHAN: Like he's gonna finger-paint it with his blood?

TEX: Know how much I could get for something like
that on E-Bay?

GABBY: Mister Quintana? Can you hear me?

(No response)

GABBY: Mister Quintana? Julian?

ETHAN: He's in orbit, man. Can't hear shit.

TEX: Maybe he can, just so whacked out he can't communicate. *(To* JULIAN*)* You're safe. You're at Ethan's house on El Centro... It's gonna be okay.

ETHAN: This isn't a house, it's a bungalow.

GABBY: Like he cares either way?

ETHAN: My name is Ethan. *(Speaks slowly)* Ethan.

TEX: I'm Tex. It's a total fucking honor to meet you Mister Quintana.

GABBY: And I'm Gabriel. We're filmmakers.

ETHAN: Just like you!

TEX: Minus the success and accolades of course.

ETHAN: But creatively. Talent-wise, we're just like you.

TEX: Total fucking geniuses.

GABBY: It'll be even more apparent when we make a film.

ETHAN: We did.

GABBY: I mean an actual feature-length film. *(Pause)* Something really sucky musta happened.

*(*JULIAN *moans. They all act like this means he is now aware—the following is overlapped and should be all but unintelligible for the audience:)*

ETHAN: *(Overlapped)* Hey, can I ask you a question? Because I direct. Nothing feature length yet, but I do have this provocative film, *Barking Spiders*, that we're trying to get off the ground. But, I'm wondering, what's your shooting ratio? I mean, like, in those long dialogue scenes you do?

GABBY: *(Overlapped)* It is so cool how you just threw out that Syd Field bullshit. Fuck the three act structure! Fuck the paradigm. Fuck plot points and all that hack Hollywood shit! Film should be art, right? Not some fucking cooking recipe!

TEX: *(Overlapped)* And the way your characters don't just try to suck the audience off. I hate it, every fucking movie tries to make you love the main characters. That whole sympathetic character myth! Characters should be compelling, not necessarily sympathetic. Right? You are so—

ETHAN: You guys HOLD ON! Don't overload him. Let him think about my question.

(JULIAN mumbles something.)

ETHAN: What was that? I didn't hear.

(JULIAN lapses back to moaning. GABBY picks up the prescription bottle.)

TEX: What's it for?

GABBY: Don't know...Zyprexa?

(GABBY throws the bottle to TEX. TEX reads it, shrugs. Can't make sense of it either.)

(They all look at JULIAN: wounded, sobbing, disoriented, and oh, so fucking pathetic. And to make things even worse, he suddenly goes into a grotesque spasm!)

GABBY: Holy shit!

TEX: What's happening?

ETHAN: He's gone spasmodic! Get me that!

(Whatever TEX grabs should be funny—maybe it's a remote control clicker? A rolled up Variety? Either way, TEX hands it to ETHAN...he leaps on JULIAN and jams it between JULIAN's teeth so he doesn't bite his tongue off. They all join in, hold him down until the spasm passes.)

(They let him go. Stand back. Long pause)

ETHAN: We should do something.

TEX: Yuh-huh.

GABBY: Cops?

TEX: Yeah. And an ambulance.

(They stare some more.)

ETHAN: He needs medical attention.

GABBY: Most definitely.

(Nobody moves.)

TEX: Well?

GABBY: Hold on.

ETHAN: What.

GABBY: We should explore our options here.

ETHAN: What options? The guy is mangled...

GABBY: Well, we call an ambulance, and they take him away.

TEX: Right.

GABBY: We become heroes and he feels obligated to screen our short and give us a deal.

TEX: With housekeeping.

ETHAN: And a discretionary fund.

TEX: Fuckin' A! Rock n' roll! Who gets to make the call?

GABBY: Hold on. All of that is a big, fat, "maybe." Maybe he feels obligated to screen our short. Maybe he helps us out with some sort of deal. Maybe.

ETHAN: Okay...

GABBY: Then again, maybe he feels obligated, he requests a tape, his assistant screens it instead, gives him coverage. The "blah, blah, blah."

TEX: Right.

GABBY: We don't know.

ETHAN: Huh.

GABBY: Point is, once he leaves our possession, it's business as usual.

TEX: And in H-town that means grab your ankles and whistle the *Jaws* theme.

ETHAN: So what are you saying we do?

GABBY: *(Over "...saying we do?")* Just go with me a moment, I'm just "pitching" this...

ETHAN: Yes.

TEX: Go on.

GABBY: I say we clean him up, show him our movie, we show him *Barking Spiders,* cement a relationship on some level, then we get him some help.

(TEX and ETHAN ponder this.)

ETHAN: In some circles, that could be viewed as morally questionable behavior.

TEX: What're we doing wrong? He's not that messed up.

ETHAN: Okay...but, and I'm only raising this to put it out there, but what if he...kinda dies?

TEX: Nobodies gonna die, come on...

ETHAN: He's got blood coming out his ear-hole right there.

TEX: Why are you trying to complicate things? He's got some scratches and bruises. No big deal. And if he really wanted, he could leave. *(To JULIAN)* You want to go? Do you want us to take you to a hospital?

(JULIAN groans.)

TEX: Sounded like a "no" to me.

GABBY: Mister Quintana, thanks for stopping by, it was a big honor to meet you, but we'd like you to leave now. *(Beat)* Please leave. *(Beat)* You're trespassing.

TEX: See? It's practically a home invasion.

(A pause)

GABBY: I don't think we should ignore the religious ramifications of this either.

ETHAN: Religious?

GABBY: Hello? I ask for divine intervention and Julian Quintana appears. Now, I'm not into that whole "god" thing, but fuck, guys, how can we ignore it?

(JULIAN groans again, starts to twitch.)

TEX: Pro'ly needs his meds. Or he could just be trippin' on black tar.

ETHAN: Or pulling a "Kidder".

GABBY: A wha—?

ETHAN: A Margot Kidder? Remember years back, some old people found Margot Kidder scrounging around their back yard, totally freaked, thought the C I A was trying to steal her brain? Some nervous episode breakdown or something. She was eating garbage.

TEX: Who's Margot Kidder?

GABBY: She played Lois Lane in the first Superman flick.

ETHAN: The one with Christopher Reeves.

GABBY: Or...another thought: He could be pulling a "Downey". Yeah. Some couple came home one night and found a drugged-out Robert Downey Junior snuggling in their bed.

ETHAN: We could be looking at a "Kidder" with "Downey" overtones.

TEX: So what's the big play? Punt and pray, or a bold offensive drive and a big score?

(Pause)

GABBY: Okay, I'll admit it, this is totally wrong, totally exploitative, and yet, I truly think it's not only the best move we could make at this point in our careers, but also, we've pretty much got a mandate from god.

(TEX and ETHAN think about this a moment.)

ETHAN: Theoretically, I see one tiny snag in this idea.

TEX: Jesus, what now?

ETHAN: Doesn't seem in any condition to watch a movie. Not even in the short term.

GABBY: That's actually a good point. He's a mess.

TEX: Then we wake his ass up. C'mon, people, let's start thinking outside the bun.

GABBY: So, okay, he's fucked up...groggy...he needs a jolt.

TEX: Like coffee, wait no—espresso. A double. A grande, venti, fuckin' something—

ETHAN: This is beyond coffee.

TEX: What we need, fellow geniuses, is crank. Hard core, mega crank.

GABBY: That'll get him up.

TEX: Keely.

GABBY: Exactly. Ethan goes to Keely's and gets whatever stimulants we can. *(Beat)* It's a plan, and at this point, it's the best we got. All right?

TEX: Shit yeah!

(GABBY an TEX both notice ETHAN hasn't chimed in.)

GABBY: What?

ETHAN: I'm just tryin' to think.

TEX: Dude, about what? This is a white-hot concept available on both D V D and BlueRay!

GABBY: What's your issue?

ETHAN: Just seems like we're going in a direction here...

GABBY: Yeeees?

ETHAN: And we should figure out some of the ramifications of what we're doing.

TEX: You want ramifications? A fucking movie deal! Raging success! Millions of dollars. Unchecked power! Red carpets. Schmoozing with the other hip, cool, elite motherfuckers! The ability to complain about the pressure of making two films back-to-back! We'll all finally be real people! And best of all: the chance to return home like fucking GODS!

ETHAN: You're right. I'm in.

(GABBY *takes a big, deep breath.*)

GABBY: So. We're going to keep America's hippest, coolest, most ironic auteur sobbing and bleeding on the couch, bump him up with drugs until he's coherent enough to watch our short and make all our dreams come true?

ETHAN: That's the plan in broad strokes.

TEX: I give it "two thumbs up."

ETHAN: Way up.

(*They stare at* JULIAN; *all three glassy eyed with visions of total fucking world domination.*)

(JULIAN *twitches, gurgles, then quietly vomits on himself.*)

(*This doesn't faze them a bit.*)

(*Intermission*)

END OF ACT ONE

ACT TWO

(Later that night. GABBY *and* TEX *with a wash rag, busy cleaning* JULIAN *up. They've already put Band-Aids on his cuts and scrapes. They've also managed to get him into a* Where Rats Go To Die *tee-shirt.)*

TEX: *(Re:* JULIAN's *looks)* What d'you think?

GABBY: Not exactly his finest hour, but it'll do. *(She finds a comb, starts fixing* JULIAN's *hair.)*

GABBY: How's that look?

TEX: Like ass. This guy is a totalfuckinggenius, he deserves a hair-style that reflects as much.

GABBY: Okay, relax.

TEX: Oh! Wait. Major idea! We put him in a dress.

GABBY: You're not fucking him.

TEX: WHAT??? No. What? It's for black mail. Photos! Intimate snapshots! He gets uppity later, it puts us in a very strong position to negotiate.

GABBY: Tex, please.

TEX: It's a choice concept.

GABBY: It's demented.

TEX: We're splitting hairs?

GABBY: That's way too Abu Ghraib-y.

TEX: I'm only saying: protect our product. Have a back up plan. Insurance.

GABBY: No way. I'm drawing the line.

TEX: Fine. Whatever. But we should at least nab some photoes. For us. Souvenirs.

GABBY: That I can live with.

TEX: Right on. Hold up. *(He looks around for* ETHAN*'s camera. It's on his desk. He nabs it.)*

GABBY: *(Re:* JULIAN*'s hair)* Better?

TEX: It'll do. *(Finds camera)* Bingo. Okay, you first.

GABBY: He needs shades. The "stunned bovine" look does not work for him.

TEX: Nice call. *(He snags some shades off* ETHAN*'s desk. Puts them on* JULIAN.*)*

GABBY: Let's do it.

*(*GABBY *fixes her hair, slides onto the couch with* JULIAN. *She puts his arm around her.* TEX *aims the camera, but keeps moving to different angles.)*

GABBY: I said "let's do it!" C'mon!

TEX: I'm composing.

GABBY: Jesus, just snap one off.

TEX: Wait a minute.

GABBY: Tex...!

TEX: I just got a brilliant idea.

GABBY: TAKE THE PICTURE FIRST!

*(*TEX *takes the picture.* GABBY *let's her smile relax.)*

TEX: I got a brilliant idea.

GABBY: I've heard enough of 'em tonight.

TEX: No—we should film this.

GABBY: Film what? We just took a—

TEX: No! This. Right now. You, me, Tex and Julian. We set up a camera there, we film this. This is a movie. This should be OUR movie!

GABBY: More.

TEX: Think about it. Three guys find a superstar having a nervous breakdown in their back yard.

GABBY: Okay, granted, that's a decent set-up. But where does it go?

TEX: Wherever it's going now. It'll be like a *Dogma* 95 thing. We'll market this as a cross between a *Dogma* film and like, some *Blair Witch-Cloverfield* thing.

GABBY: My problem with that?

TEX: Yeah?

GABBY: Nobody wants to watch a film about Hollywood wannabees.

TEX: Why not?

GABBY: Because...it's too...self-referential and narcissistic.

TEX: Dude, every other show on cable is about Hollywood. *Extras*. Fucking *30 Rock*...

GABBY: Movies should be about real life.

TEX: But this *is* real life. Our real life. This is our truth.

GABBY: But people won't care. Trust me, none of us are remotely sympathetic enough to carry a film. Especially you.

TEX: Ouch.

(ETHAN *enters holding his backpack and a brown bag.*)

TEX: Hey, man!

ETHAN: What's this?

GABBY: Just taking some pictures. Me and my close personal friend, Julian Quintana.

TEX: Dude I have another genius idea.

GABBY: He wants to film this and make this our movie.

ETHAN: How about we not incriminate ourselves with a video, okay? If we wanna convert this experience later, after things've turned out in our favor...fine. But until then: We are not filming this.

TEX: But—

ETHAN: NO! That's a rookie move. No more cameras. We all understand?

TEX: Yeah.

ETHAN: Gabb?

GABBY: Hey, it wasn't my idea. You get the stuff?

TEX: Keely coke us out?

ETHAN: Yes and no.

GABBY: Tell us the "yes" part first.

ETHAN: Keely wasn't there.

GABBY: Didn't I ask for the "yes" part?

ETHAN: ...So I got what I could. Was just her roommate...

TEX: The fox with the buzz?

ETHAN: Tanya?

TEX: Angry punker chick?

ETHAN: No. Long black hair.

TEX: Hostile chicks are erotic. Why is that?

GABBY: Who cares!?

ETHAN: A smorgasbord. (*He dumps the contents of his backpack onto the coffee table: pills, powder and vials. He takes a sixer of Red Bull from the brown bag.*)

(TEX *grabs one of the Red Bulls.*)

TEX: Sweet.

ETHAN: Hands off.

GABBY: What is all this?

ETHAN: Tanya didn't know where Keely keeps product so I just bought whatever they had—their personal stash. Some crystal and some coke. I think there's some ADD meds too.

GABBY: *(Points to some pills)* And that?

ETHAN: Viagra.

GABBY: Viagra's considered a stimulant?

TEX: For balls it is.

ETHAN: I figure, just get as many as possible in case one doesn't work.

GABBY: He can't smoke anything in his condition. Let alone snort.

(A beat as they all consider this.)

ETHAN: I knew we were moving too fast! You're right. We're screwed!

TEX: It's simple. Take everything, throw it in a blender. We make some, like, devious little smoothy from hell. Problem solved.

GABBY: Okay, but still—how we get him to drink up?

TEX: Classic beer-bong action. *(To* ETHAN*)* Still got the face hugger?

ETHAN: Damn straight. Closet.

TEX: Problem solved, people. Pour it down his throat. Just like those fuckin' ducks. Isn't that how they make paté? Or is that geese?

GABBY: Can meth and coke even be absorbed like that?

TEX: Oh, totally.

GABBY: Really?

TEX: I hope.

ETHAN: Could it kill him? I mean, swallowing pureed coke can't be healthy.

TEX: Look, the film biz is full of risks...and one of the worst is being force-fed a wild drug cocktail by a group of intense film-making geniuses. Now, let's get moving.

GABBY: All right, all right, gimme that stuff, I'll do the honours. (*She gets the drugs and pills, grabs the Red Bull and goes into the kitchen.*)

TEX: (*Closes his eyes*) Keep your cool... We're doing this... It's gonna happen... Success is part of my life. It's achievable, it's real and it's happening to me right now. And more important: I deserve it more than the next guy.

(TEX *opens his eyes to find* ETHAN *staring at him.*)

TEX: I'm getting into my "success corridor".

ETHAN: Nice.

(*In the kitchen,* GABBY *goes about setting up the blender, etc.*)

(JULIAN *twitches a bit, seems to mumble something.*)

TEX: What is it with him?

ETHAN: Whatcha' mean?

TEX: ...That gives him so much talent?

ETHAN: We got talent.

TEX: Well, duh, yeah, I know. We're totalfucking-geniuses. But still. You know what I'm saying.

(*Silence*)

ETHAN: Yeah.

(GABBY *has poured the coke, the meth, a lot of Viagra, some cold medicine and three Red Bulls into the blender. She turns it on.*)

TEX: So what is it? With Julian, it seems so...effortless.

ETHAN: I remember the first time watching *Rats*. Just the impact of that muscular dialog... The inventiveness... The... The balls...

TEX: A breath of fresh air in a world of stale blockbusters and kiss-ass comedies.

ETHAN: So cool... Five crooks with code-names based on cheese types, trapped in a warehouse...

TEX: Mister Munster...

ETHAN: Mister Cheddar...

TEX: Mister Provolone...

ETHAN: My favorite part is when Roy Scheider...

TEX: ...As the hard-as-nails Mister Mozzarella...

ETHAN: ...Yeah, when Roy figures out who the undercover cop is, pulls his gun and says—

(*They enact the classic Tarantino/John Woo "two guys aiming guns at each other's face" pose.*)

ETHAN & TEX: "Your story is full of holes, Mister Swiss!"

ETHAN: Then fills him with lead.

TEX: That was wicked-cool.

(ETHAN *and* TEX *both stare at* JULIAN *as their smiles fade.*)

(GABBY *enters with the blender full of pureed drugs and Red Bull.*)

GABBY: Okay, here it is.

TEX: I'll get the bong. (*He scrambles up and goes into* ETHAN's *bedroom.*)

ETHAN: This is our last chance.

GABBY: I know it is.

ETHAN: No. I mean...to back out.

GABBY: Oh.

(TEX *enters with a beer bong made to look in some way like the "face hugger" from* Alien.)

ETHAN: We can still...just take him outside and leave him somewhere. I'm just saying.

TEX: Ethan: It's "Harvey Keitel time". It's *Bad Lieutenant*. It's Harvey whimpering and dancing naked. It's intensity and dedication to an ideal.

ETHAN: Hey, I'm ready. I'm just making sure you guys are. Let's do it.

(ETHAN *nods for* TEX *to put the beer bong in* JULIAN'S *mouth. He does.* GABBY *takes a moment, gives the other guys a look, then pours the hellish brew down* JULIAN'S *throat.* JULIAN *swallows a bunch then sputters.* GABBY *stops pouring.* JULIAN *gurgles a bit. Moans a tad. Then seems normal.*)

GABBY: More.

(TEX *puts the bong back in* JULIAN'S *mouth.* GABBY *pours the rest in until he sputters. Again, except for a little coughing...* JULIAN *seems unfazed...and still out of it.*)

(*To put it another way: Jack shit happens.*)

(*They all wait anyway. Expectant*)

(*Still, nothing happens.*)

ETHAN: Back to square one.

(*But hold on—*)

(JULIAN *groans! A shudder goes through him! And then, slowly, he gets a massive erection! —Needless to say, it*

dwarfs ETHAN's *meager offering from the start of the play.*
The erection will last for the rest of the play.)

GABBY: Well, hello there.

ETHAN: I thought Viagra takes time to work.

TEX: Maybe it's a coke-bone.

*(And then...*JULIAN's *entire body vibrates, he grits his teeth*
like he's being wracked by extreme pain, his hands dig into
the couch.)

ETHAN: This doesn't look good...

TEX: Relax, it's fine...

GABBY: I think he's in pain...

TEX: —Just waking up. It's cool. This is a good thing.

JULIAN: AAAAAAAAAAGGGGGG!!!!

ETHAN: Julian?

JULIAN: GGGGGgggggggGGGGGGUUUUUU!!!

ETHAN: Julian, you okay?

TEX: His system's kicking in...

GABBY: Christ, his eyes are rolling back...

TEX: I'm sure it's totally normal.

GABBY: He's foaming...

TEX: That's not foam, it's spital, there's a difference.

*(*ETHAN *peers closer at* JULIAN.)*

(Closer)

(Closer)

(Suddenly, JULIAN's *arms lash out, grab* ETHAN *by the*
throat, throttles him.)

ETHAN: WOOOOOOOOAAAAAAAACCCCKKKKK!!!!

JULIAN: AAAAAAAAAAAAARRRRHHHH!!!!

GABBY: HEY!

TEX: WHOA!!

GABBY: STOP HIM—

(GABBY *and* TEX *back away in shock, stunned and frozen by the sudden viciousness of the assault.)*

*(*ETHAN *tries to defend himself, but it's impossible:* JULIAN *attacks like an amped-up force of nature, now smashing his head into the floor— Whack! Whack! Whack! Whack! Whack! Whack! Whack!)*

GABBY: DO SOMETHING!

*(*TEX *snaps out of it, grabs an empty beer bottle and smashes it over* JULIAN*'s head. No effect.* TEX *grabs another empty— smashes it over* JULIAN*'s head.* JULIAN *continues throttling* ETHAN. TEX *finds one more—smashes* JULIAN *a third time! Nothing)*

TEX: FUCK!

GABBY: HE'S GONNA HURT HIM!

TEX: *(Looking for something else to use as a weapon)* I CAN SEE THAT!!

*(*GABBY *takes a step towards the fight, talking as if trying to control a pet.)*

GABBY: Stop! Stop that! Julian—no! NO!

(ETHAN goes slack. JULIAN doesn't stop.

(Whack! Whack! Whack!)

GABBY: TEX!!!!!

*(*TEX *gives up his weapon search and dives on* JULIAN*—they grapple, but* JULIAN *has now started to tire,* TEX *manages to get* JULIAN *into a restraining hold.)*

TEX: GET ME SOMETHING!!

GABBY: Like what?

TEX: Rope!

GABBY: Where?

TEX: Fuck! A cord! Anything!

(GABBY exits, comes back with a bathrobe tie. TEX grabs it, ties JULIAN's wrists together. TEX drags JULIAN to the couch. He sits there, sweating, panting, eyes closed. TEX keeps an eye on JULIAN while GABBY runs to ETHAN.)

TEX: He okay?

GABBY: Dunno—shit...Ethan? Ethan!

(GABBY feels for a pulse. Long pause)

TEX: What?

GABBY: I don't feel anything.

TEX: There's no way.

GABBY: Feel then—I don't know—maybe I'm missing it—

(TEX goes to ETHAN, listens for a heartbeat. Feels for a pulse. Listens to ETHAN's chest again. TEX's face goes white. He backs away.)

TEX: Oh fuck oh fuck OH FUCK! OH FUCK OH FUCK!

(TEX explodes in primal rage, throwing shit around, kicking furniture, tearing magazines, pulling books from the shelves—basically trashing the set as much as the intense, method actor we've cast can. In stark contrast to TEX, GABBY just slumps to the floor, maybe she's crying, maybe she's in shock. Hell, maybe her mind just snapped. Either way, neither of them are the same. Finally, when TEX tires of beating the crap out of the room, he falls on his ass. Beat)

TEX: *(Numb)* My big bro is dead.

GABBY: *(Numb)* My future husband...

TEX: He's never gonna direct a movie...like ever. I'll never hear his pretentious voice on a D V D commentary track.

GABBY: We were gonna get married. We were gonna have kids.

TEX: That fucker believed in me. He bought me my first copy of Final Draft.

GABBY: Killed by the most talented director of our generation.

TEX: I thought Ethan was the most talented.

GABBY: We'll never know. Maybe he was.

(A long pause. Something else dawns on them—)

TEX: ...We are so fucked...

GABBY: What're we gonna do?

TEX: No idea...

(They stare at ETHAN's *corpse.)*

GABBY: Look at that blood. It's so real, it...it actually looks kinda fake.

TEX: I think I'm gonna chuck...I AM gonna chuck! *(He exits to bathroom. An instant later we hear horrific retching.)*

*(*GABBY *goes to kitchen, gets the whisky, pours a shot into a coffee cup. Drinks)*

*(*TEX *enters wiping his face with a dirty tee shirt.)*

GABBY: What now?

TEX: There is no "what now". It's over, chick. Fade to black. Begin end credits. El finito bandito. *(Takes a deep breath)* But I do know this: The International Laws of Vengeance dictate I now kill this guy. No matter how much I respect his talent. Julian Quintana must die. *(Looks around)* I need something heavy. Or sharp. Preferably something heavy and sharp.

GABBY: Wrong.

TEX: Wrong? What the fuck do you mean wrong?

GABBY: You're not killing him.

TEX: Dude, he offed my fucking brother! He murdered your possible future husband!

GABBY: Hey, I know all that! You don't think I don't!?

TEX: I don't know what you're thinking!

GABBY: There's a big picture here—

TEX: Yeah. There is a big picture. And it's called *The Godfather.* That's right, it's *Godfather* time. *Godfather*s one, two and yes, even the vastly underrated and far superior *Godfather Three.* Vengeance.

(GABBY *stares between* JULIAN *and* ETHAN. *An odd look of dertermination washes over her.*)

GABBY: No. It's gut-check time. You need to pull your shit together.

TEX: There is no shit left to even try and pull together. Ethan is dead. His body is right there. Don't you fucking care? He LOVED YOU WOMAN!

GABBY: Tex. I blew a sixteen-year-old tonight. Technically that makes me a sexual predator. Instead of being horrified, your brother, who supposedly wanted to marry me, would have let me give the kid a full-on fuck session if he thought it'd get us a film deal.

TEX: So—like that's bad? He was thinking of you! Of your career. You've got a selfish streak in you, you know that? A real selfish streak.

GABBY: He wasn't thinking of my career. He was thinking of his. And now, so am I.

TEX: I still need to kill him. I'm sorry. (*He finds something big to bash* JULIAN's *skull in.*)This'll work.

GABBY: You think if Julian killed you, Ethan would make a blood feud out of it?

TEX: Hell, yeah.

GABBY: Not a chance.

TEX: Dude, I'm his golden goose. I'm the genius behind *Barking Spiders*.

GABBY: In the end, to him, you're relationship wasn't as brothers, but as director and writer. And that makes you as expendable to him as any other hack in this town.

TEX: LIES! *(He approaches* JULIAN.*)*

GABBY: Tex! Don't do it! Don't fucking do it. We can turn this whole thing around!

*(*TEX *looms over* JULIAN *with his weapon.)*

GABBY: You can still get payback without killing him! You've heard it before: Success is the best revenge! We can use Julian! Like parasites! Ethan would want it that way. We can't bring him back, but we can make sure he didn't die in vain.

*(*TEX *yells, throws his weapon aside, and flings himself onto the ground, pounding the floor with his fists. When he's done, he just lays there, face down. Long pause)*

GABBY: Tex?

TEX: Hm?

GABBY: Are you ready to celebrate your brother's memory by continuing forward with the project he has now died for?

*(*TEX *sits up. Something's dead inside.)*

TEX: Yeah. Okay.

GABBY: So let's sort through some ugly facts. It's not gonna be fun, but we need to make things clear as we plan our next move.

TEX: Fine.

GABBY: You ready to do this?

TEX: I'm ready.

GABBY: One: Ethan is dead.

TEX: Yeah.

GABBY: We can call the authorities, but not only would that mean we'd have to explain some morally dubious career choices, but we'd also be depriving the world of Hollywood's edgiest living director. And even if it didn't play out that way, keep in mind one thing...

TEX: What?

GABBY: Quintana is rich.

TEX: Check.

GABBY: Very rich. He could afford a Big Time Lawyer. And what would his defense be? Not his fault. Why? Because we gave him a cocktail of illegal substances. They'll pin it on us. However, I doubt Quintana will be in any hurry to confess.

TEX: I'm with you.

GABBY: So I say this: we stick to the original plan. We show him the movie. Tell him we'd like a nice little production deal.

TEX: With housekeeping.

GABBY: Yeah.

TEX: And a discretionary fund.

GABBY: Sure.

TEX: What about Ethan?

GABBY: From this point on, there is no more Ethan.

TEX: No?

GABBY: No.

TEX: Then what's that?

GABBY: A corpse. Ethan is inside us now. Right here. *(Points to her heart)* That's what the human heart is, Tex.

A little studio apartment where beautiful memories live.

TEX: The human heart is a little studio apartment?

GABBY: Yeah. That's right.

TEX: Is it rent controlled?

GABBY: What?

TEX: Is the little studio apartment in my heart rent controlled?

GABBY: I...ah...

TEX: I GOTTA KNOW! For Ethan's sake...

GABBY: Yeah. Of course.

TEX: My bro will always be with me?

GABBY: Yes. He'll be with both of us. What now lies on the floor here....is just the body of an extra.

(Pause. Tex thinks about this.)

TEX: How do we get rid of this...this extra's corpse, then?

GABBY: What do you think the L A River's for? Strip him, stuff his underwear in his mouth, drop him in, he washes up in a week as another unsolved murder. This is the serial killer capital of the world, let's use L A's natural resources.

TEX: What if there's no water in the L A River?

GABBY: Okay. We take him down to fifth and Spring... Skid Row...we prop him up against the wall...it'll be days before anyone realizes he's dead and by then all kinds of homeless guys will have looted his body and contaminated the evidence.

TEX: What evidence?

GABBY: Whatever. I don't know. I don't watch C S I.

(TEX *shakes his head, blinks a few more times. Something seems to dawn on him.*)

TEX: Whoa, fuck!

GABBY: What?

TEX: I just get the feeling this is the kinda stuff that can get you sent to hell.

GABBY: God created adrenaline for situations like this. I suggest you get yours pumping. There will be a time and place for grief, remorse, and spiritual concerns. That time is not now. In or out?

TEX: In. But I'm only doing this for Ethan.

GABBY: We both are.

(JULIAN *groans.*)

GABBY: Okay, here's the plan: Get Ethan out of here.

TEX: I'm not touching him.

GABBY: You're dragging him into his bedroom for the time being. I'll secure Julian better in case he decides to freak again.

(TEX *just stares at* ETHAN'*s body.*)

GABBY: Get moving!

(TEX *snaps into action, drags* ETHAN *into the bedroom.* GABBY *rips a cord from the stereo and binds* JULIAN'*s legs. Makes sure the bindings on his arms are tight.*)

(*During the following monologue,* JULIAN *slowly starts to become more coherent.*)

GABBY: Sorry about this kiddo, but I'm just following the road map. I mean, hell, think about it. I ask the Big Director for Divine Intervention and what happens? You show up. There is no way this is not part of some huge cosmic plan. You know? It's just too impossible to fathom such a coincidence. There are forces at work here; powerful, mysterious, beautiful, sexy, Jared

Leto caliber forces reaching down from the heavens
and moving us around like chess pieces. I feel like
we're actors trying to fulfill the directors vision. And
what is god but like, a Speilberg or Coppola but with
just a totally bigger budget and final cut? I hope you
understand why we've had to do things this way.

(JULIAN *stares forward, glassy eyes, awake but out of it. He
nods vaguely.*)

(TEX *enters.*)

TEX: Okay, okay, what now?

GABBY: Show time. Get *Barking Spiders.*

(TEX *goes to a shelf, searches, finds a copy of* Barking
Spiders *burned onto a D V D.*)

TEX: Here we go.

(GABBY *slaps* JULIAN *slightly on the cheek to makes sure
he's paying attention.*)

GABBY: Okay, now, Mister Quintana—can I call you
Julian? Would that be cool?

JULIAN: Yuuuu? (*He looks at* GABBY. *Nods. Drools a bit*)

GABBY: Great, so then, um, Julian, I guess there's
nothing else to say...

(TEX *goes to the T V, puts the disk in.*)

TEX: Sit back, relax, and enjoy the mind-blowing genius
that is—*Barking Spiders.*

(TEX *hits play.* JULIAN *stares forward at the T V.* GABBY
bites her lip with anticipation.)

(Barking Spiders *begins...*)

(*Lights fade. In the dark, we hear bits of "Barking Spiders."
Note to sound design person: There Will Be Farts.*)

END OF ACT TWO

ACT THREE

(The flickering T V light rises. We hear end credit music playing. TEX *gets up, turns on the light.)*

*(*TEX *and* GABBY *look at* JULIAN, *unable to hide their expectation.)*

TEX: So, Julian, that was it. That was *Barking Spiders*. The Directors Cut.

GABBY: It's the only cut.

TEX: But when you say "Directors Cut" it sounds so much cooler.

GABBY: What'd you think?

(Long pause. JULIAN *looks around, seeming a little less dazed.)*

JULIAN: The...fuck...am I?

GABBY: We've been over that.

JULIAN: Who... Who are... Who are you?

GABBY: C'mon, Julian. What did you think about our movie?

(Long pause. JULIAN *looks down at his erection.)*

JULIAN: My...dick hurts.

TEX: You've been going through a rough patch, but it's all getting better now.

JULIAN: I'm...my hands...I'm...tied up... Why do I have a

boner?

GABBY: Now, I noticed you didn't laugh once, but I know—at least this is how I am—I don't do that whole "out loud" thing. I never even crack a grin. I mean, I can be totally loving a movie or whatever, and like think it's super funny and all, but on the outside, you'd never know. Is that your deal?

JULIAN: Someone...take...these off me...and call a doctor...

TEX: What did you think, Julian? Stop teasing. Give it to me straight. One maverick to another.

JULIAN: Who...the fuck...fuck are you?

TEX: I'm Tex. This is Gabby. Like we already said.

JULIAN: Day...

TEX: What?

JULIAN: Day!

TEX: I don't—

JULIAN: What day is it?

TEX: Uh...

JULIAN: What's the date?

TEX: The seventh.

JULIAN: Seventh...seventh...shit...last I remember it was...I think, the twenty-fifth or...something. I was at a party. Eli's. Eli's thing. Yeah, and...what? Linda and Cassie. And...we're in the bathroom...then nothing. So where am I again?

TEX: Ethan's bungalow.

JULIAN: Ethan...? Who...?

TEX: Never mind.

JULIAN: Phone.

TEX: Wha—?

JULIAN: I need a phone.

GABBY: It's broken.

JULIAN: Where's mine?

GABBY: You didn't have one.

TEX: You were in the Dogloo, man. You were in an intense state of emotional turmoil so we brought you inside for care and shelter.

JULIAN: My head is on fire. My dick feels like a fucking banana that's gonna rip out of its peel...

TEX: Ouch.

JULIAN: ...I remember...or dreamt...

GABBY: What?

JULIAN: I...think I...remember...

TEX: Yeah?

JULIAN: I attacked...viciously attacked...a clown...then something going down my throat. Is that right?

GABBY: Pretty crazy.

JULIAN: This shit is digging into my wrists...

GABBY: Look, Julian, I'm gonna be honest with you here. You've been acting in an extremely volatile manner. Okay?

TEX: Like violently volatile.

GABBY: I think it's best to just keep you restrained for a little bit until we're sure you're not gonna have any more episodes. Be a danger to yourself and others.

TEX: We're thinking about your own safety.

GABBY: Absolutely.

(JULIAN *thinks a moment. Blinks. Brain and wits not too sharp.*)

TEX: Now...we just showed you our movie. Your eyes were open, okay, maybe a little glassy, but you seemed to be awake. Did you see it? You only puked once...I take that as a positive sign...

JULIAN: That thing I was watching...

GABBY: Yeah.

JULIAN: That was a movie?

GABBY: A short, but yeah.

GABBY: We, uh, put it together to attract investors.

JULIAN: You made that?

GABBY: Yeah. The three of us.

TEX: Two.

GABBY: Right, right, the two of us.

JULIAN: So I wasn't hallucinating?

GABBY: What d'you mean by that?

JULIAN: That thing I just had piercing my brain?

TEX: Dude, you are so funny. Seriously.

JULIAN: So...you're not...

TEX: C'mon dude, for reals what did...

JULIAN: Can I have some water?

TEX: You got it.

(TEX *goes into the kitchen.* JULIAN *does his best to comprehend his situation.*)

JULIAN: You know...you're really making me work too hard for...I'm not in any kind of critical zone where I should be giving opinions on anything...

GABBY: Listen to me: You're Julian Quintana. You're the fucking beacon for everyone like me.

JULIAN: Like you? Like you how? What're you like?

GABBY: People who've spent their youths chasing the film mirage.

(TEX *comes back in.*)

TEX: Here you go.

JULIAN: Thanks.

(TEX *holds the glass for* JULIAN *while he sips.*)

TEX: So c'mon. Stop being coy. What did you think?

JULIAN: ...About your film?

TEX: Tell us. Yes. Fuck yes.

GABBY: Please. What we do with our futures...the rest of our existence...depends on it.

(*A long pause. Then:*)

JULIAN: It was really fucking funny.

TEX: You serious?

JULIAN: It had an edge to it. An honesty. And yet it was sexy too. And those fart jokes really gave it that extra oomph.

TEX: Fart jokes are my specialty. You know that that's what a Barking Spider is. A fart.

JULIAN: Yes. I know.

TEX: Sorry. Go on.

JULIAN: Each joke worked, alright? Not a fart joke too far. You took us to the fart edge...and just...balanced us there. And you gotta understand, I am in no way into the whole "gross-out" comedy genre. But...

GABBY: You really liked it?

JULIAN: Yeah. Yes. Absolutely. (*Beat*) Very, very much. (*Beat*) Exciting work. (*Beat*) Now maybe you can let me off this couch?

GABBY: What kind of advice can you give us...

JULIAN: Advice...?

TEX: Like, if you had made this, but you knew what you know now, what would be your move? Because, truth? We've sent it to all the major festivals and jack shit...

JULIAN: This isn't a festival movie, alright? Not even close.

TEX: No?

JULIAN: It's not pretentious. There's no angst ridden lesbians. No disaffected white kids shooting heroin. No precious and whimsical outsiders fighting against the boring suburbs.

TEX: Hell no.

JULIAN: I would try to get it to someone who could really champion a piece of material like this.

TEX: Like you?

(JULIAN *has to think about that one.*)

TEX: How 'bout it stud? Come aboard as executive producer?

GABBY: Tex...

TEX: No, seriously. Would you consider it? "Julian Quintana presents: *Barking Spiders*."

(JULIAN *tilts his head to the left, to the right, thinking it over...*)

JULIAN: Sure.

GABBY: You would?

TEX: He just said...

GABBY: You'd take *Barking Spiders* to your people?

JULIAN: Sure. Lawrence would probably laugh his ass off at this.

TEX: FUCKING AWESOME!

JULIAN: Can I get up now? This is really killing my circulation bad.

TEX: Dude, totally.

(TEX moves to untie JULIAN.)

GABBY: You...really liked it?

JULIAN: Absolutely. You both are clearly huge talents. *(Looks at his crotch)* Maybe one of you should call 9-1-1. My joint's not going down...

(Beat. TEX has stopped untying JULIAN.)

JULIAN: C'mon... Get these off of me. *(Silence)* What're you waiting for?

TEX: What'd you just say?

JULIAN: Get these off me?

GABBY: No. Before.

JULIAN: What? You guys are huge talents? I meant that. You are. Huge goddamn talents. Clearly.

(TEX and GABBY share a dread-soaked look.)

JULIAN: What...

GABBY: We're not letting you up until you tell us the truth.

JULIAN: I did.

TEX: Bullshit! We know all about industry double-speak!

JULIAN: You're making no fucking sense.

GABBY: Then give it to us straight.

JULIAN: I did. Untie me.

TEX: Julian, did you like it or not? Fucking be honest, man. You owe us that. You fucking owe us!

(JULIAN gives him a look.)

TEX: Okay. Maybe you don't. Be honest anyway.

JULIAN: Untie me.

TEX: I'm not comfortable with that.

JULIAN: You want the fuckin' truth. Untie me.

(Beat. TEX looks at GABBY. She nods. TEX unties JULIAN.)

JULIAN: Can I get some more water?

(TEX goes into the kitchen, gets some bottled water.

(JULIAN massages his wrists. He adjusts his massive boner.)

JULIAN: I'm gonna need a doctor for this beast...

(TEX returns with the water. JULIAN downs the entire bottle in one gulp.)

TEX: So? *(Pause)* TEX: Let's hear it.

(Pause.)

JULIAN: It fucking sucked, alright? On every level possible. The cinematography, the shot selection, the use of the frame. The dexterity with the camera makes Kevin Smith look like Kubrick. If any of you spend another day of your life under the illusion that you have any future in film, you're wasting your life. Every moment you live here struggling, you're pissing any hope of an honest existence away. You will never make it. You're fooling yourself. You're not even good enough to be a straight-to-video hack. Take the lamest, brain-dead comedy... And I'm talking the Wayans Brothers or anything from the post *Saturday Night Live* crowd... And it's better than this. Do you understand me? You're a screenwriter? Please. You're a typist. You put ink on paper. Go away. You guys are just gumming up the works. Every project you submit makes it that much harder for the truly talented to get their script or film through the pipeline. Your quest to make it isn't noble. It's sad. You're like a cat trying to bury a shit on a marble floor—

(TEX *snaps: he leaps at* JULIAN, *totally bugging out, pounds his face, kicking, clawing, slapping him in a burst of total cinema-geek rage.*)

(GABBY *jumps on* TEX, *desperately trying to pull him back. He turns on her, throws her violently into the wall—she hits it head-first and crumples to the floor. He goes back to beating* JULIAN.)

(*After a disturbing amount of time, he finally stops.*)

(JULIAN *isn't moving.*)

TEX: (*Breathing heavy, there's something off about him now...yeah, I know there was something off after Ethan died...but now it's at an even deeper level.*) There you go. The explosive and shocking burst of violence that's become your trademark. Unfortunately, I can't think of any funny little quip to soften things with, but hey, that's real life for ya. How's it feel? Huh? That was for Ethan. (*Beat*) I'm the total fucking genius. You just got lucky. You're no better than me, asshole. Not one bit. (*Spits on him*) Best of luck with your career. (*He stares at* JULIAN's *body. Maybe checks out the blood spatter on his own shirt. Maybe he giggles ever so slightly.*)

(*From outside, we hear the warped* Hurray for Hollywood *jingle from the ice cream truck...the distorted song will warble in the background for the rest of the play.*)

TEX: Three A M. And that goddamn ice cream truck is still trundling around out there. (*He goes to the front door, opens it, then stops in his tracks, stunned. Awed, as if seeing a holy vision*) Holy shit. You won't believe this... Dennis Woodruff is out there. He's buying a Choco Taco. Angelyne's there too. Just pulled over in her pink Cadillac. What are the odds? (*Beat*) I'm gonna go join 'em. Talk shop. One H-town playa to another. Wanna come, Gabbs? (*Beat*) Gabbs?

(GABBY *doesn't answer.* TEX *doesn't seem to care.*)

TEX: Whatever. We'll catch up later. *(Out)* Yo, Dennis! D-Man! Angelyne. What's up? Where's the party? *(He exits.)*

(The warped Hurray for Hollywood *music rises a bit. Then the white square of projector light snaps on and all other lights black out. We hear the projector with the flapping film strip.)*

(Slowly, GABBY *pulls herself to her feet. Blood trickles from her hairline. She walks towards* JULIAN's *body, staggering a bit. She turns him over. He still has his uber erection.)*

GABBY: *(Numb/dazed)* It's all gonna work out...it's gonna be okay...you hear me Julian? You hear me, Mister Quintana? You came here, were sent here...to save me. And maybe...maybe in my own little way, I'm gonna save you...help you with your ultimate creation. *(She pulls her dress up, climbs on top of him...mounts him.)* Oh, yeah...that's it...I can't be here...and not...I gotta be here...and contribute... And not just...in development or something... I must create. You understand that, don't you? We're all geniuses...we're all grappling with the same shit... *(She grinds away on top of him as she speaks.)* I...guarantee you Julian, your fertile seed won't get stuck in development hell. No, Julian, your sperm is getting my green light. I'll give birth to the coolest, hippest, most ironic baby the world has ever known. The future of independent cinema will emerge from my womb; a sticky, screaming, creative ball of energy wrapped in celluloid placenta...ready to pursue his singular vision. It's so clear to me now...so...so fucking clear...I'll name him...Edgy. Edgy Quintana. *(Out, to the audience)* How cool is that?

(White projector light blacks out. All we hear: the flapping film in the dark, then that cuts out. Silence. Fin)

END OF PLAY

9 780881 455175